ILLUSTRATOR'S NOTE

This is a participatory Russian folk tale I learned while growing up in Russia. In the story, different animals—from the tiny to the enormous, from the vulnerable to the ferocious—come to live together. There are several variations of the tale. In one, the animals live in a large mitten. In another, they live in a jar. Here I use my favorite, in which the animals inhabit a little hut in the woods. In Russian the hut is called a *teremok*, which is a diminutive of *terem*—a fancy traditional Russian house. What I and all Russian children treasure most about the tale is the way children and parents can act out the story together, with the children knock-knocking and announcing themselves in different animal voices. But as an adult, I also see the story as an allegory of the collapse of the Soviet Union and the socialist ideal of disparate peoples living peacefully together.

With thanks and love to Alex, my husband, critic and devoted nudge

The art for this book was prepared first as black line drawings. These were used as guidelines for the full-color art, which was painted with watercolors. The line drawings were then photographed separately for greater contrast and sharpness.

Published in the United States by North-South Books Inc., New York.
Published simultaneously in Great Britain, Canada, Australia, and New Zealand by North-South Books, an imprint of Nord-Süd Verlag AG, Gossau Zürich, Switzerland.

Library of Congress Cataloging-in-Publication Data is available.
A CIP catalogue record for this book is available from The British Library.
ISBN 1-55858-329-7 (trade binding)
ISBN 1-55858-330-0 (library binding)
1 3 5 7 9 TB 10 8 6 4 2
1 3 5 7 9 LB 10 8 6 4 2

Designed by Marc Cheshire

KNOCK, KNOCK, TEREMOK!

A Traditional Russian Tale · Adapted and Illustrated by

KATYA ARNOLD

NORTH-SOUTH BOOKS / NEW YORK / LONDON

A Fly was flying in the sky.
She came across a little hut.
Knock, knock, knock.
Who lives in the teremok?
Nobody answered.
So she made the house her home.

A Mouse was running in the field.
She came across a little hut.
Knock, knock, knock.
Who lives in the teremok?
It's me, the Fly, queen of the sky.
Who are you?
I am the Mouse, who needs a new house.
Let's live together.

A Frog was leaping through the field.
He came across a little hut.
Knock, knock, knock.
Who lives in the teremok?
It's me, the Fly, queen of the sky.
It's me, the Mouse, who needs a new house.
Who are you?
I am the Frog, from out of the bog.
Let's live together.

A Duck was walking through the field.

He came across a little hut.

Knock, knock, knock.

Who lives in the teremok?

It's me, the Fly, queen of the sky.

It's me, the Mouse, who needs a new house.

It's me, the Frog, from out of the bog.

Who are you?

I am the Duck, who has good luck.

Let's live together.

A Hare was hopping through the woods.
He came across a little hut.
Knock, knock, knock.
Who lives in the teremok?
It's me, the Fly, queen of the sky.
It's me, the Mouse, who needs a new house.
It's me, the Frog, from out of the bog.
It's me, the Duck, who has good luck.
Who are you?
I am the Hare, who jumps in the air.
Let's live together.

A Fox was strolling through the woods.
She came across a little hut.
Knock, knock, knock.
Who lives in the teremok?
It's me, the Fly, queen of the sky.
It's me, the Mouse, who needs a new house.
It's me, the Frog, from out of the bog.
It's me, the Duck, who has good luck.
It's me, the Hare, who jumps in the air.
Who are you?
I am the Fox, in nice white socks.
Let's live together.

A Pig was walking in the woods.

She came across a little hut.

Knock, knock, knock.

Who lives in the teremok?

It's me, the Fly, queen of the sky.

It's me, the Mouse, who needs a new house.

It's me, the Frog, from out of the bog.

It's me, the Duck, who has good luck.

It's me, the Hare, who jumps in the air.

It's me, the Fox, in nice white socks.

Who are you?

I am the Pig, who can dance a jig.

Let's live together.

A Wolf was marching through the woods.

He came across a little hut.

Knock, knock, knock.

Who lives in the teremok?

It's me, the Fly, queen of the sky.

It's me, the Mouse, who needs a new house.

It's me, the Frog, from out of the bog.

It's me; the Duck, who has good luck.

It's me, the Hare, who jumps in the air.

It's me, the Fox, in nice white socks.

It's me, the Pig, who can dance a jig.

Who are you?

I am the Wolf, the nice little Wolf!

Let's live together.

So they did!
And everyone was very happy.

A Bear was stomping through the woods.
He came across a little hut.
Knock, knock, knock.
Who lives in the teremok?
It's me, the Fly, queen of the sky.
It's me, the Mouse, who needs a new house.
It's me, the Frog, from out of the bog.
It's me, the Duck, who has good luck.
It's me, the Hare, who jumps in the air.
It's me, the Fox, in nice white socks.
It's me, the Pig, who dances a jig.
It's me, the Wolf, the nice little Wolf!
Who are you?
I am the Bear, and I need a new lair.
May I live with you?
No, there is no room—go away!
But may I stay on the roof?
No, you're too heavy.
No I'm not, let me try.

So the Bear sat on
the house and squashed it.